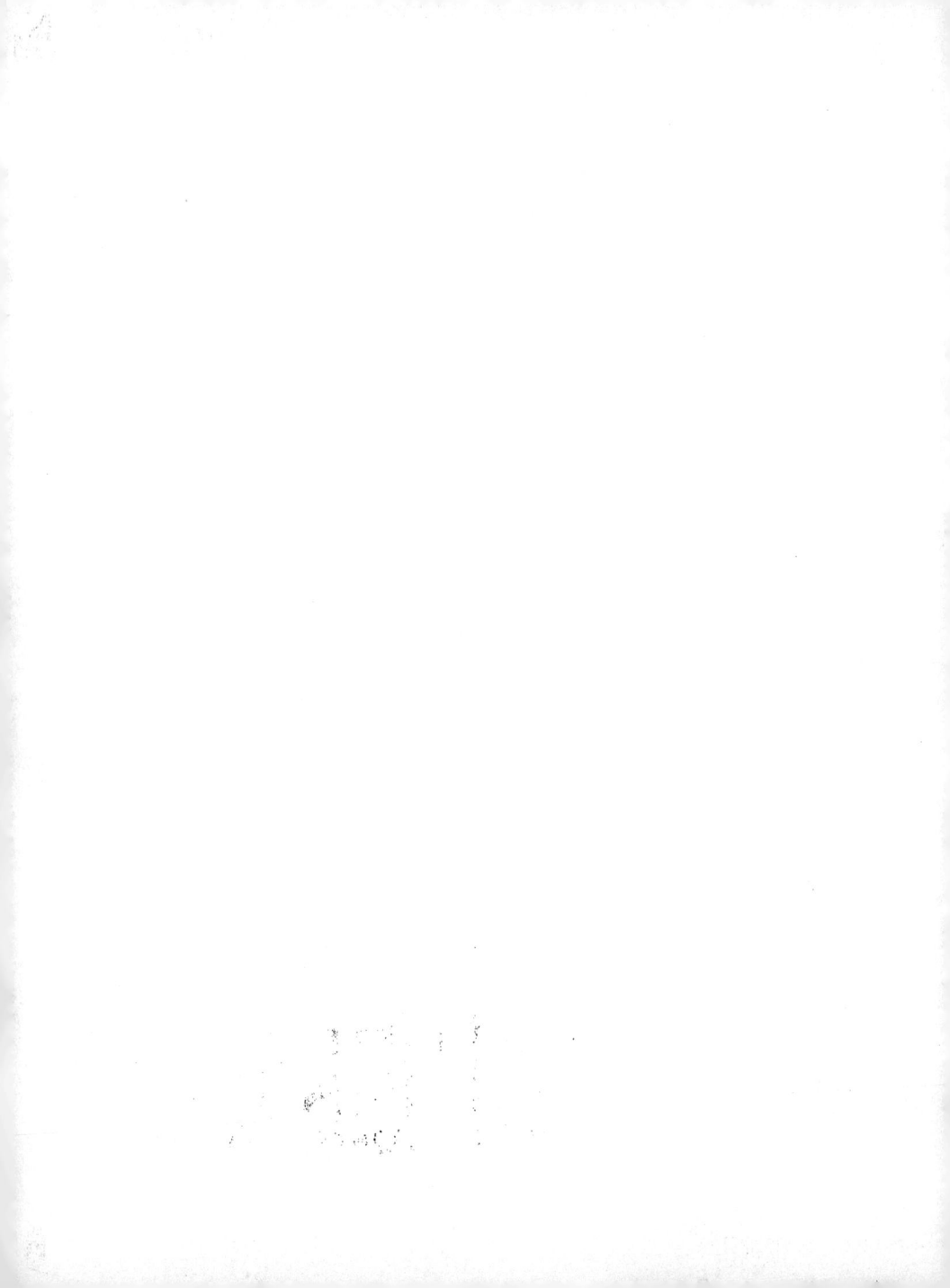

Stories
Jesus Told

Retold by Owen Cole and Judith Lowndes
Illustrated by Roger Payne

Heinemann Educational Publishers
Halley Court, Jordan Hill, Oxford OX2 8EJ

MADRID ATHENS PARIS
FLORENCE PRAGUE WARSAW
PORTSMOUTH NH CHICAGO SAO PAULO
SINGAPORE TOKYO MELBOURNE AUCKLAND
IBADAN GABORONE JOHANNESBURG

© Heinemann Educational 1995

First published 1995

95 96 97 98 99 10 9 8 7 6 5 4 3 2 1

British Library Cataloguing in Publication Data
A catalogue record for this book is available from the British Library

Starter Pack
1 of each of 12 titles: ISBN 0 435 01066 2

Library Hardback Edition
Stories Jesus Told: ISBN 0 431 07757 6
1 of each of 12 titles: ISBN 0 431 07763 0

Designed by Sue Vaudin; printed and bound in Hong Kong

Acknowledgements
Back cover photograph:
Sonia Halliday Photographs

Jesus lived a very long time ago.
He told people lots of stories to
help them learn about God.
Jesus wanted people to know that
God loved them.

Later, the stories were written down.
We can read these stories in a
special book.
It is called the Bible.

Here are three stories Jesus told.
They are about things that were lost
and then found again.

The Lost Sheep

A man had a hundred sheep.

He looked after them in the fields.

One of the sheep got lost.

What do you think the man did?

The man went off to look for his sheep.

He left all his other sheep behind.

He looked and looked for the lost sheep.

At last the man found it!

He carried it home.

He was very happy.

8

The man asked all his friends to
come and see.
He said, "Look! I lost my
sheep and now I have found it.
Let's have a party!"

The Lost Coin

There was once a woman who
had ten silver coins.
One day she lost one of her coins.
She was very sad.

The woman lit a lamp to
shine in all the dark corners.
She got a brush to sweep the floor.
She looked and looked for her coin.

At last she found her coin.

She went to all her friends.

She said, "I am so happy.

Let's have a party!"

The Lost Son

There was once a man who had two sons.
They helped him with his work.

One of the sons said to his father,
"May I have the money that
you have been keeping for me?"

14

The father gave his son the money.

The son went far, far away.

He spent all the money.

He had no money.

He had no food.

He had no friends.

He was very sad and very lonely.

The son went back to his father's house.

He was sorry that he had gone away.

He was sorry he had spent the money.

His father saw him coming.

He rushed up to meet him.

He said, "I am so happy you

have come back!"

18

The father said, "We must have a party!
Get my son some new clothes.
Get some food ready for the party."

The other son was working in the fields.
When he came back to the house he
saw his brother at the party.
He was very sad.

His father said, "Why are you sad?

The man's brother said, "I have

stayed with you.

I have worked hard.

You have not had a party for me."

His father said, "You have always been here with me.
I know that you are safe.
I share everything with you."

Then the father said, "Your brother was
lost and now he has been found.
We were sad, but now we can be happy!"

Jesus told these stories to help
people understand that
God loves everyone.